How to be Brilliant at

RECORDING IN SCIENCE

Neil Burton

 Brilliant Publications

We hope you and your class enjoy using this book. Other books in the series include:

Science titles

How to be Brilliant at Science Investigations	978 1 897675 11 3
How to be Brilliant at Materials	978 1 897675 12 0
How to be Brilliant at Electricity, Light and Sound	978 1 897675 13 7
How to be Brilliant at Living Things	978 1 897675 66 3

English titles

How to be Brilliant at Writing Stories	978 1 897675 00 7
How to be Brilliant at Writing Poetry	978 1 897675 01 4
How to be Brilliant at Grammar	978 1 897675 02 1
How to be Brilliant at Making Books	978 1 897675 03 8
How to be Brilliant at Spelling	978 1 897675 08 3
How to be Brilliant at Reading	978 1 897675 09 0
How to be Brilliant at Word Puzzles	978 1 897675 88 5

Maths titles

How to be Brilliant at Using a Calculator	978 1 897675 04 5
How to be Brilliant at Algebra	978 1 897675 05 2
How to be Brilliant at Numbers	978 1 897675 06 9
How to be Brilliant at Shape and Space	978 1 897675 07 6
How to be Brilliant at Mental Arithmetic	978 1 897675 21 2

History and Geography titles

How to be Brilliant at Recording in History	978 1 897675 22 9
How to be Brilliant at Recording in Geography	978 1 897675 31 1

Christmas title

How to be Brilliant at Christmas Time	978 1 897675 63 2

Published by Brilliant Publications,
Unit 10, Sparrow Hall Farm,
Edlesborough,
Dunstable,
Bedfordshire,
LU6 2ES

Sales and stock enquiries:
Tel: 01202 712910
Fax: 0845 1309300
e-mail:brilliant@bebc.co.uk
www.brilliantpublications.co.uk

General information enquiries:
Tel: 01525 222292
The name 'Brilliant Publications' and its logo are
registered trademarks.

Written by Neil Burton
Illustrated by Kate Ford
Cover photograph by Martyn Chillmaid

Printed in the UK

© Neil Burton 1995
ISBN 978 1 897675 10 6

First published in 1995
Reprinted 1995, 1997, 1998, 2000, 2003, 2007
10 9 8 7

Contents

Introduction

How to be Brilliant at Recording in Science contains 38 photocopiable ideas for use with 7-11 year olds (plus two for teachers to use). The book contains structured worksheets aimed at developing a systematic approach to investigating in science. The format for recording suggested here is based upon the premise that the work should be practical and related to children's own ideas and understanding. *How to be Brilliant at Recording in Science* is designed to be highly compatible with National Curricula throughout the United Kingdom.

Each worksheet is designed to have a particular skills focus and we recommend that you read through the teacher's section before using the sheets to ensure that you choose the one most closely matching the learning objectives you have set. Also, suggestions are made for adapting particular sheets to meet the particular, differentiated needs of your pupils.

These sheets are *not* designed to be used in isolation, but to supplement any science scheme that is being used. The teacher should provide the context for the activity. The use of one or more of these sheets will encourage pupils to adopt a more structured and systematic approach to their work in science.

The worksheets in this book are subdivided into six sections:

Teacher sheets
The two sheets in this section are designed to assist the teacher in planning for pupil led investigations and to record assessments of how well individual children are meeting the learning objectives being set for them.

Thinking and planning
These sheets are designed to encourage children to think about the activity before they attempt it; to discuss and record their ideas, predictions and hypotheses; and to concentrate on the planning of particular aspects of the science activity.

Recording results
These sheets provide structured formats that are sufficiently flexible to be used in a very wide range of situations, in conjunction with sheets from the previous section.

Observation
These sheets provide formats for the recording, ordering and sorting of observations.

Presenting findings
These sheets provide a wide range of formats suitable for presenting most forms of data that can be collected from investigations.

Content specific
This section contains sheets for the recording of ideas, observations and measurements about particular scientific content areas.

Using the worksheets

Below, for each of the sheets, we identify some of the potential learning objectives that children could be steered towards.

Teacher sheets

Investigation planning sheet   page 9
To be used at the topic planning stage for the teacher to:
- identify the expected prior learning of the children;
- predict the actual activities that might be required;
- identify parts of the NC requirements.

Group assessment   page 10
To be used during discussion or observation of practical work to:
- provide a format for recording the degree to which individual children have attained particular planned learning objectives.

Thinking and planning

Brainstorm!   page 11
Children should be able to:
- demonstrate an understanding of the factors that might potentially effect the outcome of an investigation;
- share and discuss their understanding.

My ideas   page 12
Children should be able to:
- predict the outcome of an activity;
- provide adequate reasons (hypothesize) why this should happen;
- give a brief account of what actually happened.

Our ideas   page 13
Children should demonstrate the ability to:
- share and consider each other's ideas;
- arrive at a compromise, or otherwise agreed, position.

Questions!   page 14
Children should demonstrate the ability to:
- identify areas relevant to the line of enquiry;
- to phrase questions in a format that could lead to investigation.

Concept mapping   page 15
Children should demonstrate the ability to:
- identify words relevant to the area of study;
- link these words in a meaningful way to show understanding of underlying scientific concepts ('force' and 'move' could be linked together, as in: 'force' needs to be applied to make an object start to 'move').

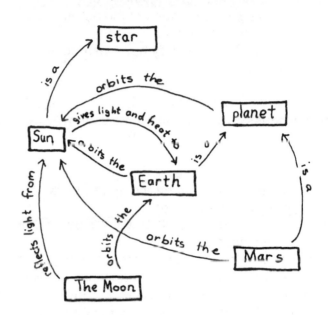

Fair test   page 16
Children should demonstrate the ability to:
- identify the factors that will be controlled to make the investigation fair;
- explain how these factors will be controlled to make the investigation fair;
- explain how the investigation will be carried out to ensure that the results are valid (indicate that the test will be repeated or carried out over a suitable period of time).

My plans   page 17
Children should produce:
- a sequenced plan for the investigation;
- a comprehensive list of equipment.

Keeping a record   page 18
Children should demonstrate the ability to:
- measure changes;
- record these measurements;
- present the data.

Measuring changes   **page 19**
Children should demonstrate the ability to:
- make appropriate choice of measuring devices.

Keeping it safe   **page 20**
Children should identify:
- the equipment they intend to use;
- the safety implications of the activity they intend to carry out;
- the safety points they have learned from the activity.

Show that I understand the process   **page 21**
Children should demonstrate the ability to:
- describe the process as a sequence of events;
- demonstrate understanding of why the process takes place;
- suggest an activity that would support their explanation.

(Processes such as evaporation, breathing, echoes, etc. could all be approached in this way, both before, and after, the subject is formally taught – any improvements in understanding can then be identified.)

This is what I know about ...   **page 22**
Children should be able to:
- demonstrate their knowledge about a particular aspect of science;
- identify potential sources of information, both primary and secondary.

Recording results
Recording sheet   **page 23**
Children should demonstrate the ability to:
- make a series of linked observations.
This is a very flexible multipurpose format designed to be used for recording changes that occur over time. Examples of contexts in which it can be used appear on page 8.

My results   **page 24**
Children should demonstrate the ability to:
- make a careful record of their results.
Differentiation can be built in by the teacher part-completing the table, with headings etc.

Science prompts   **page 25**
Children should demonstrate the ability to:
- complete a 'full write-up' of a science investigation.
We advise that this sheet is best given once the children are used to the full range of structured sheets provided here, and even then, only infrequently.

Tally chart   **page 26**
Children should demonstrate the ability to:
- record the results of surveys.

Observations
Similarities and differences   **page 27**
Children should identify:
- similarities and differences between living things, plants and phenomena.

Sort it out!   **page 28**
Children should demonstrate the ability to:
- differentiate and identify variations across a range of similar living things, materials and phenomena.

Sorting key   **page 29**
Children should demonstrate the ability to:
- identify categoric differences between a range of similar things;
- sort according to these differences;
- devise a sorting key based upon these differences;

⬭ boxes are for questions

⬭ boxes are for items

Guess what I've seen!   **page 30**
Children should demonstrate the ability to:
- identify where particular living things, materials or phenomena have been found or seen to occur.

Presenting findings
Sorting into sets, 1   **page 31**
Children should demonstrate the ability to:
- sort a group of living things, materials or phenomena into two mutually exclusive sets.

Note
Some sheets, especially group ones, can be enlarged to A3 size if you have the facilities, to allow all children to participate fully.

Using the Recording sheet on page 23

In general terms, this sheet is designed to be used to record observations over a period of time, in order to show change. The length of time between each observation will obviously vary considerably, depending on the nature of the investigation being carried out.

More able 5-7 year olds, and most in the 7-11 age group, will probably be able to cope with a blank worksheet but others may well be helped by the addition of a simple drawing in each of the sections to start them off. Below, are some suggestions of the type of investigation they could be used with.

Possible drawing on the grid

(saucepan)	**Heating water** Start with ice cubes or cold water in the Pyrex saucepan. Heat it on a 'Baby Belling' or similar hot plate. Children record what is happening in the saucepan at between 5 to 10 minute intervals.
(seed tray)	**Growing seeds** Start at the point where the first shoots break through the surface. How frequently you ask the children to update their records on the sheet will depend on what type of plant you are growing. If different groups within the class are observing seedlings growing in different conditions, it is important that all the sheets are updated at the same time so that fair comparisons can be made.
(rounders post)	**Apparent motion of the sun** There are two ways to approach this: either record the length and position of the shadow at different times during the course of a day, or record the length of the shadow at the same time of day but on different weeks.
(twig)	**Growing animals** How often you record will depend upon the animal you are observing. Those that will produce significant changes in a relatively short period include butterfly and moth larvae (where their food is available) and small numbers of tadpoles. Include a starting point on the sheet (eg a twig) to help establish a 'scale'.

Investigation planning sheet

Area for investigation	Learning objectives		Possible outcomes
Context/topic area	Ideas the children hold/ might hold	Possible activities	
Skill focus			
Content focus			
NC relevance	Resource requirements		

How to be Brilliant at Recording in Science

Group assessment

Teacher _____   Date _____

Activity _____   Class/group _____

	Objectives					Comments
Names						

Group evaluation

Brainstorm!

_____   Names _____

might depend upon…   _____

                                              _____

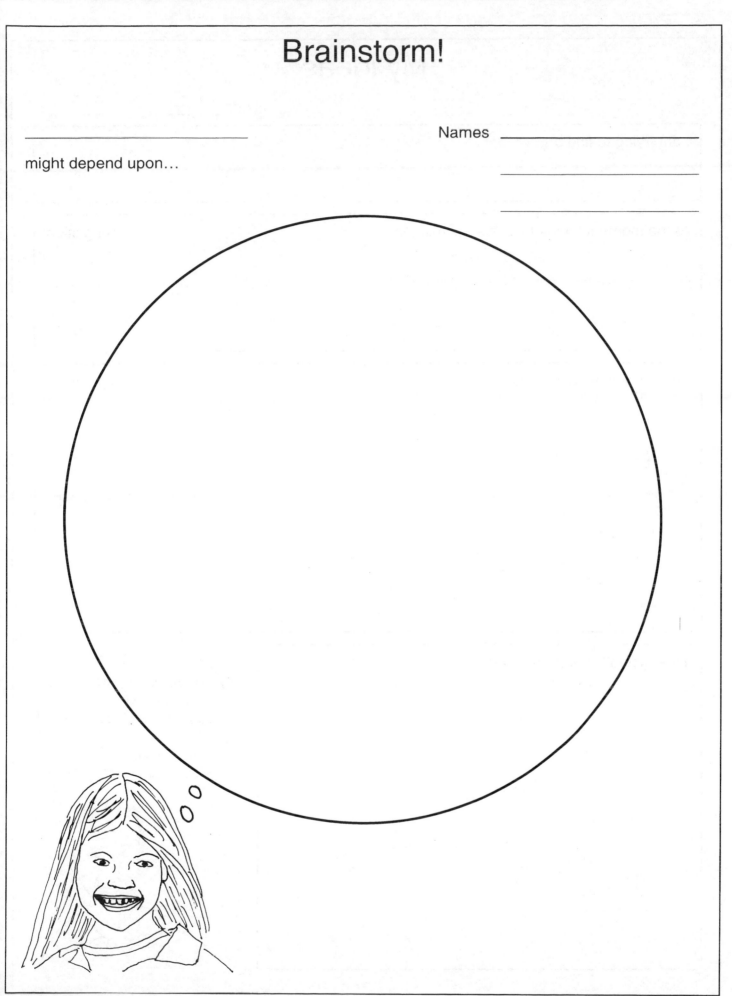

My ideas

Name _____

I am trying to find out…

At the moment I think that this will happen…   (prediction)

I think it will happen because…   (hypothesis)

What actually happened was…

Have your ideas changed at all? Talk to your teacher about what you think now.

Our ideas

_____ thinks

_____ thinks

Together we think…

_____ thinks

_____ thinks

How to be Brilliant at Recording in Science

Questions!

Names _____

We want to find out about...

Questions we would like to ask...

Which of these questions could be turned into investigations?

Concept mapping

Name _____

Here is my list of important words about… _____

My words are…

This is how they fit together…

Use this sheet to show what this topic means to you. Show that you understand what the words mean and that you can see how they are linked together.

How to be Brilliant at Recording in Science

Fair test

Name _____

I am trying to find out…

I am going to change…

I am going to measure what happens to…

To make the test fair I will…

My plans

Name_____

I am trying to find out…

This is what I am going to do…

1	2

3	4

I am going to need…

How to be Brilliant at Recording in Science

Keeping a record

Name_____

I am trying to find out…

I am going to change…

I am going to observe or measure the changes in…

by using…

I will record what happens by…

My recording sheet will look like this:

I will present my findings using a…

It might look something like this:

Measuring changes

Name _____

I am trying to find out…

I will be changing…

I will need to measure…

Measuring tools I *could* use include…

I have decided to use…

This would be the best thing to use because…

I will record the measurements…

Keeping it safe

Name_____

My investigation is about…

The equipment I want to use is…

To make sure I 'keep safe', I must remember to…

The safety points I have learnt from this activity include…

Showing that I understand the process

Name _____

This is what I know about…

This is what I think happens…

The reason I think this is because…

I could check that I'm right by doing this…

How to be Brilliant at Recording in Science

This is what I know about...

Name_____

This is what I know about...

I know this because...

I could check that I'm right by doing this...

You could use this sheet to show what you know about penguins, planets or the properties of plastic!

Recording sheet

Name _____

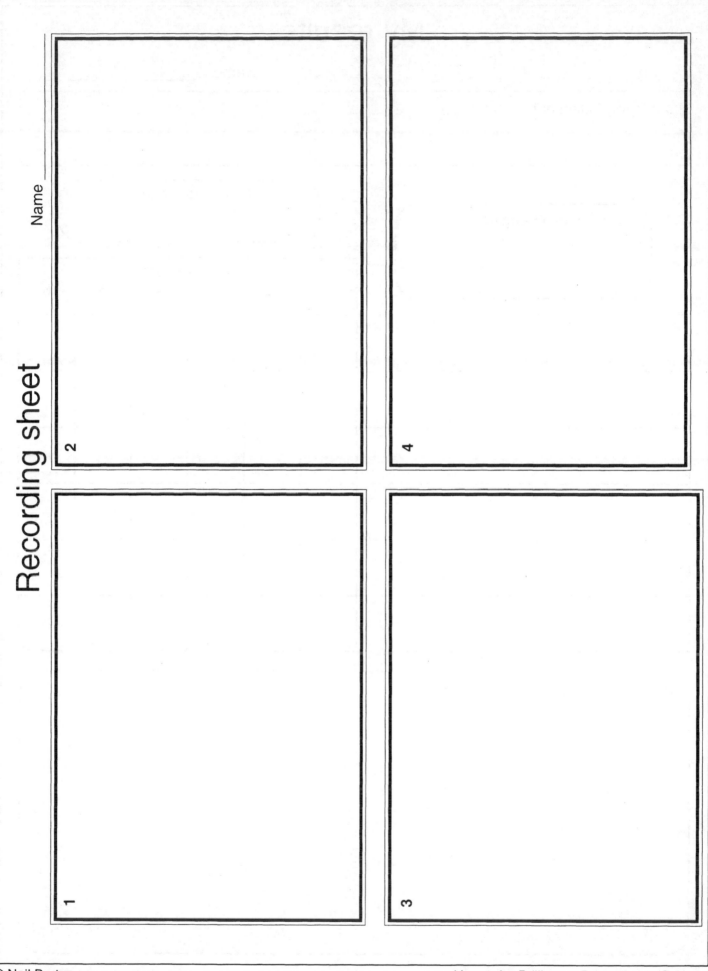

2

1

4

3

How to be Brilliant at Recording in Science

My results

Name _____

I am trying to find out…

I am changing…

I am measuring…

	Measurement					
	1	2	3	4	5	6

I am going to present these results like this:

Science prompts

Use these starting points to help you write about your science.

About the group
- Who are you?
- Who are you working with?
- What are you working on?

About your ideas
- What are you trying to find out?
- What are you going to change in your investigation?
- What are you going to measure?
- What must you keep the same to make it a fair test?
- What do you expect to happen?
- Why do you think this?
- Does anybody else in your group think differently?

About the investigation
- What are you going to do?
- For how long or how many times will you do it?
- What will you need?
- Which measuring tools will you use?
- How will you record what happens?
- How will you present your findings?
- How will you ensure that the investigation is carried out safely?

During the investigation
- Record what happens.

About your findings
- What happened?
- How does this compare with what you expected?
- What have you found out?
- Was the investigation fair?
- How could you improve on what you did?
- Have your ideas changed since starting the investigation?
- Do you have any new questions?

How to be Brilliant at Recording in Science

Tally chart

Name_____

I am carrying out a survey to find out…

I am recording the number of…

I will present this data using a…

Similarities and differences

Name _____

I am comparing _____ with _____ .

differences	similarities	differences

Underline the similarities and differences that you have identified by *observation*.

Put a star beside the things which you *know* are similar or different but could not observe.

EXTRA!
Compare your lists with someone else who has looked at the same two things.
What are the similarities and differences between the lists?

Compare your lists with someone else who has looked at two **similar** things.
Have you both been looking at the same sorts of features?

How to be Brilliant at Recording in Science

Sort it out!

Name_____

I am trying to sort...

What I am sorting	How I am sorting it					

Use this chart to record how you've sorted things. For example, minibeasts: number of legs, wings body segments...

Sorting key

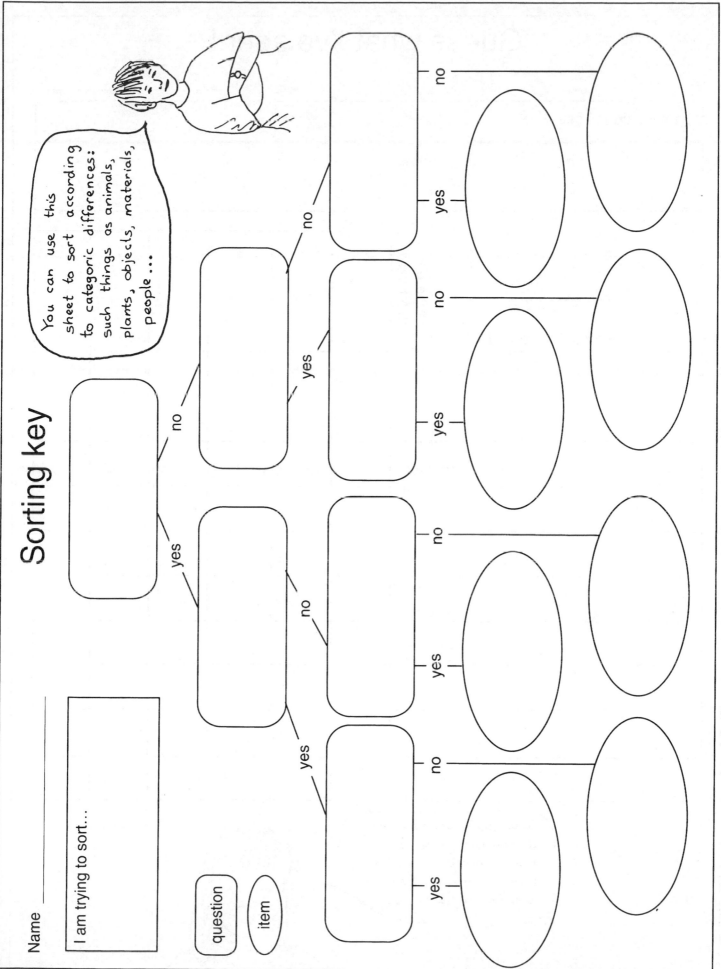

Name _____

I am trying to sort...

You can use this sheet to sort according to categoric differences: such things as animals, plants, objects, materials, people...

question

item

© Neil Burton
This page may be photocopied
for use in the classroom only.

How to be Brilliant at Recording in Science

29

Guess what I've seen!

Name_____

I am looking to see…

What I observed	Where I observed it					

You could use this sheet to record where you've found minibeasts, seen birds feeding, observed plants growing…

Sorting into sets, 1

Name _____

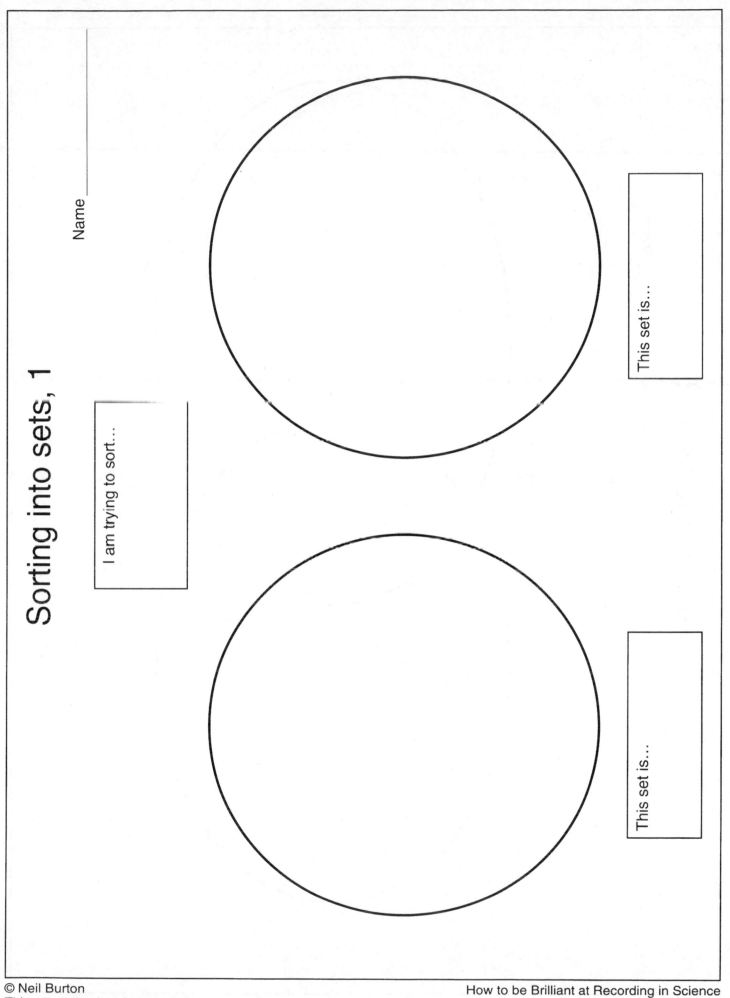

I am trying to sort...

This set is...

This set is...

How to be Brilliant at Recording in Science

Sorting into sets, 2

Name _____

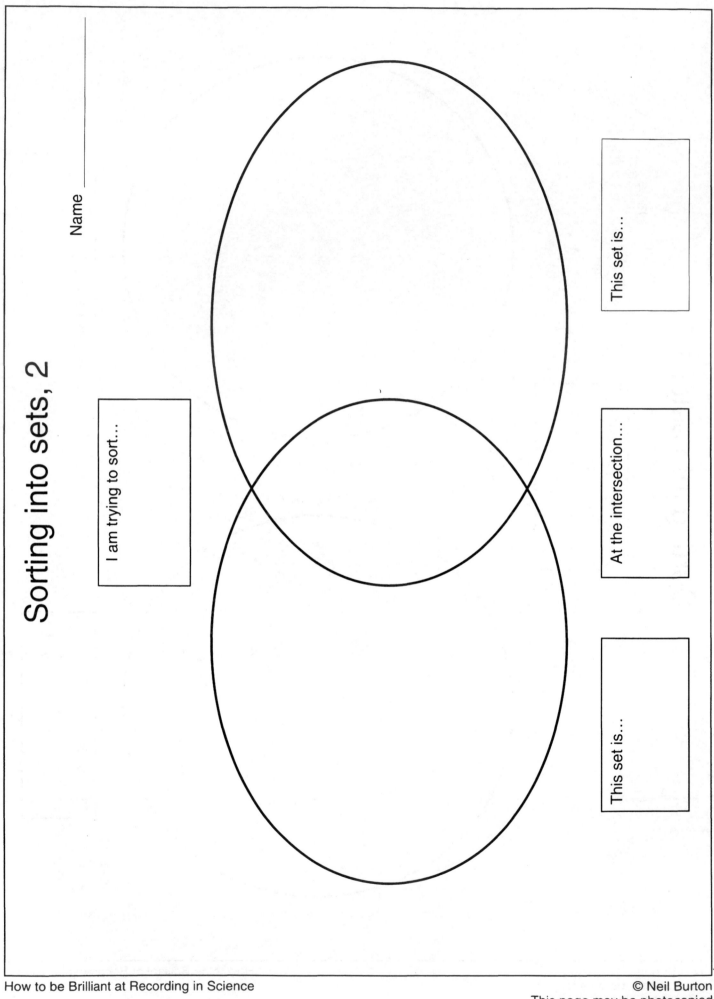

I am trying to sort...

This set is...

At the intersection...

This set is...

The Daily Scientist

Date   'The Investigator'   Price

Amazing Discovery at _____ !
by Senior reporter _____ .

How to be Brilliant at Recording in Science

Cycles

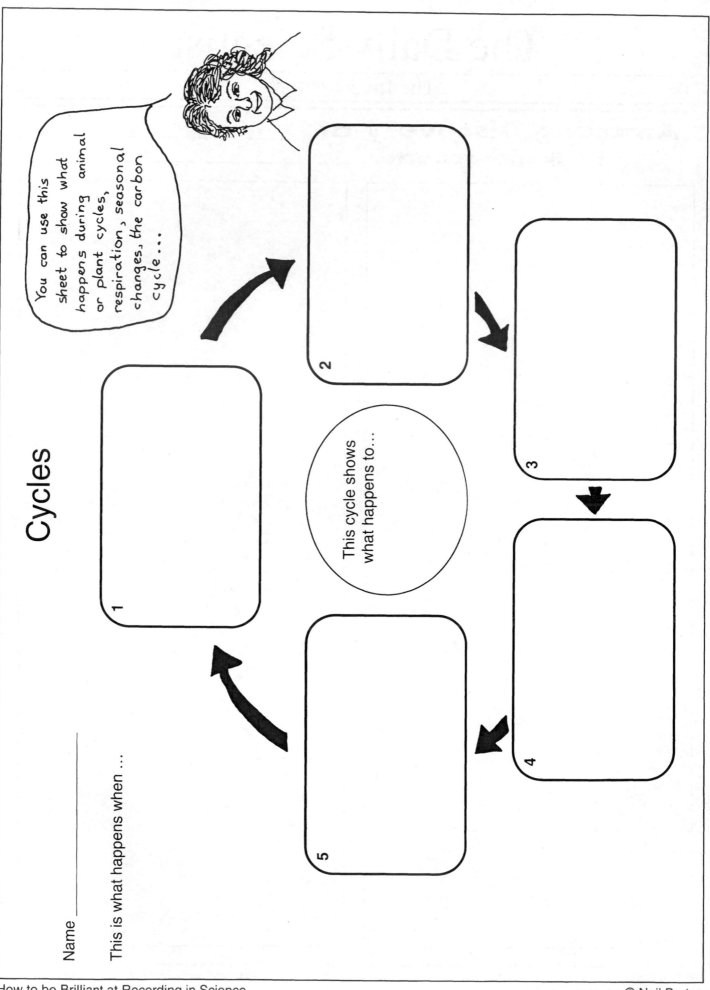

You can use this sheet to show what happens during animal or plant cycles, respiration, seasonal changes, the carbon cycle....

This cycle shows what happens to...

Name _____

This is what happens when ...

Chain

Name _____

The ———→ relationship means...

Try using relationships such as 'is eaten by', 'on heating becomes', 'is farther from the Sun than', ...

How to be Brilliant at Recording in Science

Bar chart

Name _____

This bar chart is about…

This is what I measured:

This is what I changed:

My results show that…

How to be Brilliant at Recording in Science

Line graph

Name _____

This line graph is about...

This is what I measured:

This is what I changed:

My results show that...

Pie chart

Name_____

This pie chart shows the findings from my survey of…

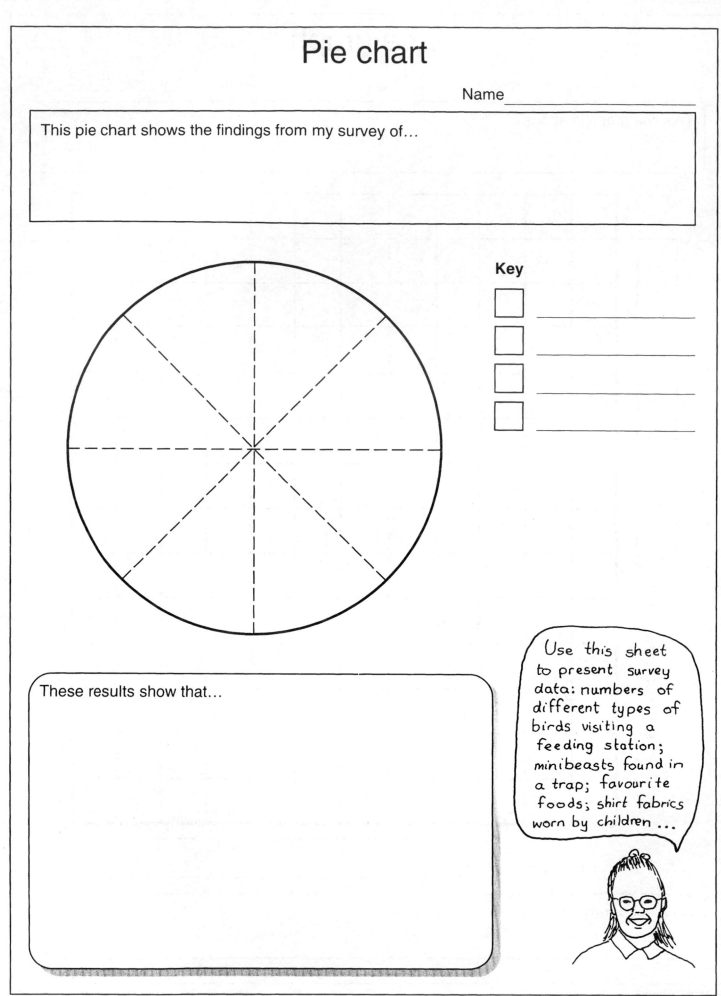

Key

☐ _____

☐ _____

☐ _____

☐ _____

These results show that…

Use this sheet to present survey data: numbers of different types of birds visiting a feeding station; minibeasts found in a trap; favourite foods; shirt fabrics worn by children …

My findings, 1

Name_____

I was trying to find out…

I predicted that…

My results show that…

How this compares with my prediction:

What I think now:

My findings, 2

Name_____

I was trying to find out…

I predicted that…

My prediction was based on the idea that…

My results show that…

I think that this happened because…

Applying and understanding

Name _____

My investigation was about…

I found out that…

This helps to explain why…

To follow up these ideas I would like to…

How to be Brilliant at Recording in Science

My minibeast

Name _____

I found it...

My description of it

_____

_____

_____

_____

_____

What it looks like

A good name for it would be...

It's real name is...

Looking through a lens I can see...

My plant

Name _____

I found it growing…

Size

Colour

Smell

What it looks like

A good name for it would be…

It's real name is…

leaf

stem

Looking through a lens I can see…

flower

Just the job!

Name _____

I'm looking for the best material to make a _____ .

	The materials I might try are…

I will need to carry out these tests…

I think _____
might be the best because…

On the whole _____
was the best because…

The case of the empty torso

Name_____

Name the organs **inside** your body. What organs have you got and where do they go?

Key	Name	Number	Key	Name	Number
☐	_____	____	☐	_____	____
☐	_____	____	☐	_____	____
☐	_____	____	☐	_____	____
☐	_____	____	☐	_____	____
☐	_____	____	☐	_____	____

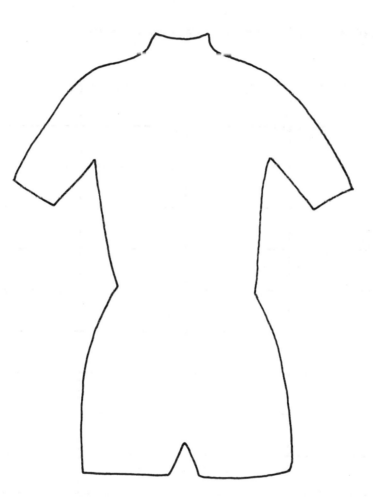

Try completing this sheet alone or in a group. Do this sheet before starting the topic, then again afterwards. How have your ideas changed?

Measuring and comparing

Name_____

After measuring my friends I want to look at relationships between…

What I am measuring				
Who I am measuring				

Use this chart as a spreadsheet to record the measurements of several different people so that the results can be compared.

I enjoy...

I am good at...

I want to get better at...

My measurements

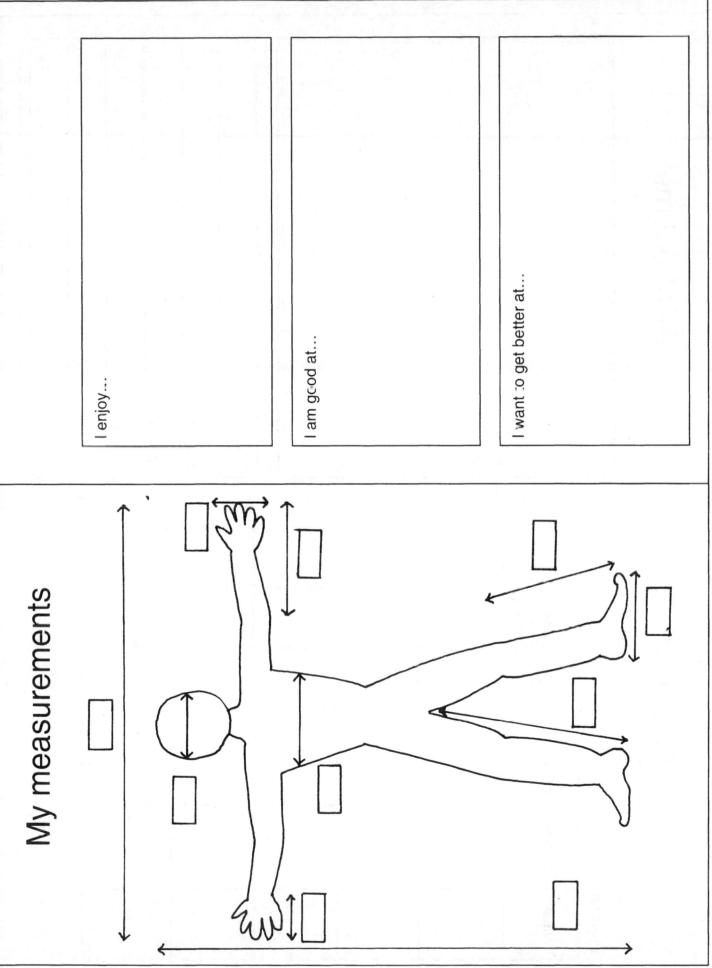

How to be Brilliant at Recording in Science

All about me!

My name is…

I was born on…

My age is…

I live at…

Getting fitter

Pulse rates

week	at rest	peak pulse	pulse after		
			1 min	2 min	4 min